Going into Darkness

To Régine and our sons

Going into Darkness

Fantastic Coffins from Africa

Text and photographs by Thierry Secretan

Thames and Hudson

Glory is the Sunlight of the Dead   **Balzac**

This obituary notice of Nuumo Kwatei Kwaku Nkpa Quartey was displayed in his native district of Labadi six days after his death. It states that the dead man was popularly known as Ataa Aku Nkpa, which means that in practice he was called Ataa Aku, 'Grandpa Aku'. The obituary then gives his age and the place and date of his death, followed by the names of his children, his sisters and his cousin.

The funeral arrangements are set out in bold type. The wake-keeping was to be held on the Friday at Agbawe, the house belonging to the old man's clan, the Agba. The burial would take place the next morning at the public cemetery, to be followed that afternoon by the funeral rites, which would continue into Sunday. The list of funeral committee members, responsible for organizing the funeral and receiving donations, ends with the traditional invitation 'All Friends and Sympathisers are invited.'

Ataa Aku was buried in a cocoa pod (see pages 42–55) as a symbol of his success in growing that particular crop.

OBITUARY

Nii Kpobi Asaawa (Agbawe Akutsotse), Nii Goji Kwatefio (Head of Otopa We) and Nii J. C. Anang (Kpobi We) announce the death of

Nuumo Kwatei Kwaku Nkpa

QUARTEY

(popularly known as Ataa Aku Nkpa)

(aged 91)

which occurred at Labadi on Monday, 19th September 1988

CHILDREN: Kwate Kwablah (Farmer, Okorso), Brother Emmanuel Kwatei Quartey (Tema Community 1 Assembly, Church of Pentecost), Ebenezer Mensah Quartey, Adjei Okpoti (P. & T. Corporation Accra), Victoria Kwale Quartey (Trader), Kwakor Kwaku Nkpa (Trader), Christopher Anum Quartey Djarshie Kwaku Nkpa (Trader) and Beatrice Tsotso Quartey

SISTERS: Madam Fofo Teiman, Ankpa Kwatiokor and Madam Nkrong Quartey

COUSIN: Madam Abisa

WAKE-KEEPING

Friday, 30th September 1988 at Agbawe, Labadi

BURIAL

Saturday, 1st October 1988 at the Labadi Public Cemetery

FUNERAL RITES

will follow immediately after burial at Agbawe

CHIEF MOURNERS

Nii Kpobi Asaawa, (Agbawe Akutsotse), Nii Goji Kwatefio (Head of Otopa We), Asafoatse Gbagbe, Nii Sowah Akrowa, Nii Anyaa Sowah, Nii Sowah Gbagbe, Nii Sowah Pono, Ataa Anang Asuom (all of Otopa We), Nii J.C. Anang (Kpobi We), Nii Sowah Gbetor (Awua We), Nii Adjei Okpoti Tawiah (Owusu We) and Nii Owu Larsey (Asua We)

WIDOW: Madam Adolefio Tetteh Din of Nii Boyefio We, Labadi

All Friends and Sympathisers are invited

PRINTED BY THE GHANA PUBLISHING CORPORATION   VICTORIABORG PRESS, ACCRA

A day will dawn when you will not see the evening

Horologium of Father Drexelius

Translated from the French *Il fait sombre, va-t'en*
by Ruth Sharman

First published in the United States of America in 1995 by
Thames and Hudson Inc., 500 Fifth Avenue, New York, New York 10110

British Library Cataloguing-in-Publication Data
A catalogue record for this book is available from the British Library

ISBN 0-500-27839-3
Library of Congress Catalog Card Number 95-60135

Printed and bound in Italy

The Celestial Family

In 1987, on the second Saturday in August, the fishing community of Botianaw in Ghana buried the oldest member of the village, Tse Obaneh, in a gigantic wooden onion. The onion, complete with roots, measured three metres (ten feet) overall and was painted the colours of a real onion. On top was the figure of a man planting his spade in a bed of six little onions. The village of Botianaw, which lies beside the Gulf of Guinea, is surrounded by onion fields, and these fields had been the property of Tse Obaneh. At eighty-three the richest man in the village had earned the title of ancestor, abandoning his earthly existence, but not his earthly relations. It was now incumbent on the living to glorify his success.

In Ghana, like most of the rest of Africa, there are no formalized funeral services. The burial of an old person in animist, Moslem and Christian traditions is closely associated with ancestor worship and is the single most important community activity, taking place every Friday and Saturday of the year. It is the ultimate manifestation of deep-rooted tradition.

Tse Obaneh's onion had been made in the workshop of Kane Kwei, a carpenter who manufactured coffins in a whole variety of shapes for the hundred or so burials that take place each year among the Ga community, the dominant ethnic group in the region surrounding the capital, Accra.

The dead are constantly present in the daily life of the Ga and no one eats or drinks without first making offerings to their ancestors. Respect for the ancient customs is a matter of life and death; a person's whole well-being depends on them, and these customs are a permanent link with the people who first established them. The Ga believe in reincarnation within the family, regarding sterility, which disrupts this process, as the ultimate misfortune. Nor can a person's spirit rejoin its celestial family or become an ancestor capable of reincarnation unless it has undergone the appropriate burial rites.[1] For a Ga it is better to incur lifelong debts than to cut back on funeral expenses.

It took five days to make Tse Obaneh's onion and twenty-four hours to bury him in this masterpiece of funerary art.

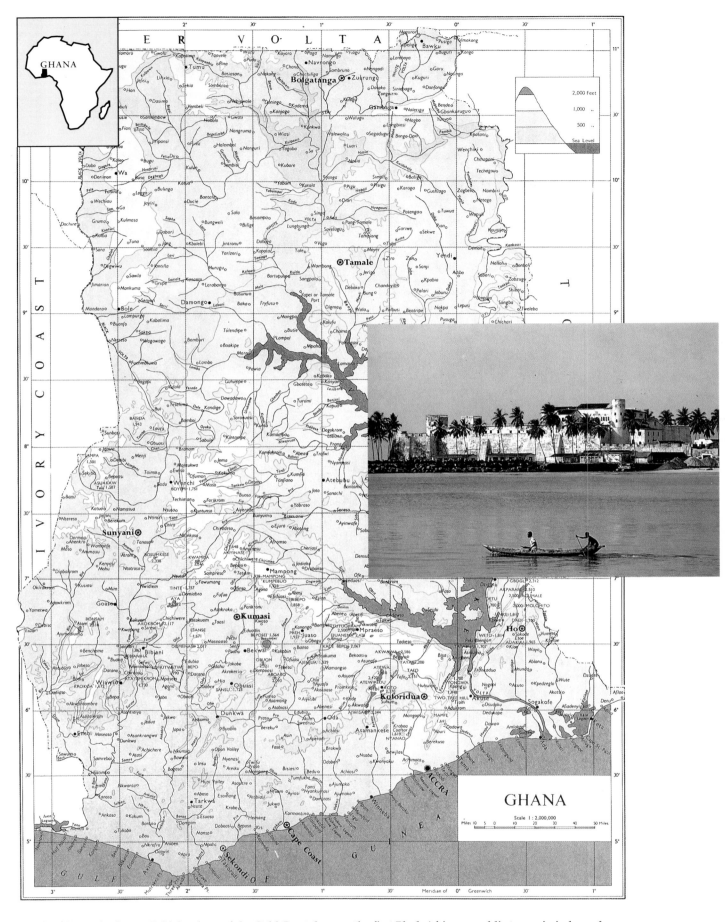

In 1957 Ghana, the former British colony of the Gold Coast, became the first Black African republic to regain independence and to change its name. The Portuguese first landed here in 1471 and began trading in gold, building a string of forts at Elmina and elsewhere along the coast to protect their interests. They were the first inhabitants of the coast to use coffins to bury their dead.

Teshi, 1987

Kane Kwei's workshop was situated at Teshi, a small fishing village on the outskirts of Accra. The display room was simply a shed with a wire-mesh front facing on to the main road. Lined up inside were a giant golden eagle, a blue tuna, a Mercedes Benz, a cocoa pod and a pirogue, a type of dugout designed for launching at high tide.

Kane Kwei strode across the courtyard separating his house from his workroom. At seventy-one he was thin and gaunt, and his fishing shorts drew attention to his emaciated legs. But he still walked with a straight back and there was a mischievous expression in his bright eyes. 'This coffin is for a fisherman', he said, resting his hands on the pirogue. 'Since this is a fishing village, I always try to keep one in stock.' Then he went over to the tuna. 'This one', he said, 'is for a fisherman with a particular knack for catching tuna.' Stepping carefully over to the eagle, Kane Kwei went on: 'The eagle[2] is generally reserved for chiefs. The Mercedes Benz is for wealthy motorists. And the cocoa pod is intended to remind us of how the dead man made his fortune.' No further explanations were forthcoming, nor were they needed: the express purpose of Kane Kwei's coffins was to glorify the dead by displaying the source of their success in life. Kane Kwei had made a sports boot for a boxer, a saw for a carpenter and an oil can for a garage owner. 'The children of a well-known university lecturer were debating what shape of coffin to choose for their father', he told me, adding with a smile: 'I suggested a parrot holding a pen in its beak.' Kane's learned parrot has since become the favourite design with the families of academics.

Kane Kwei was insistent about one thing: that his art had not evolved out of African customs or Ghanaian tradition. 'I have created every shape you can imagine,' he said, 'but the first person to make coffins like these was a man called Ata Owoo. Since I was a good carpenter, Ata Owoo encouraged me to continue his work.' Ata Owoo died in 1976 and, since Kane Kwei's accounts of the origins of this funerary art[3] varied from one meeting to the next, it was important to obtain corroboration from several other sources.

Kane Kwei

Kane Kwei was born in Teshi in 1922. In the Ga language 'Kane' means light and 'Kwei' is the name given to the fourth male child in a family. Kane's father had worked as an electrician on the country's only stretch of railway when Ghana was still a British colony known as the Gold Coast, and had earned a reputation for the excellent oil lamps he manufactured in his spare time. Teshi is one of the seven Ga 'towns' situated beside the Ocean, the others being Accra (which gave its name to the capital), Osu, Labadi, Nungoa, Tema and Kpone. Each of these townships owns a strip of land that stretches northward into an area of arid grassland and each of the villages[4] on the plain is a farming settlement attached to one or other of the seven Ga townships.

At the age of eight Kane Kwei left Teshi and went to live at Asamankese, one of the farms belonging to his clan. He returned to Teshi at the age of fourteen and went to live with Kane Adjetei, his *musumbi* or elder brother by the same mother and father, who taught him carpentry. Kane Kwei spent the next six years working with Adjetei, who told me that the younger boy showed little interest in making furniture and roofs, but was extraordinarily skilled at sculpting wood. Apparently he would chisel away in his spare time, purely for pleasure and using nothing but a knife.

In 1937 Kane Kwei went on a journey that would mark the end of his period of apprenticeship. When he left, Teshi was just a fishing village near the coast road. There was little traffic on the road – only the odd lorry or vehicle belonging to the colonial administration – and barrels of palm oil harvested on the plain were still rolled to the coast by hand.

Accra, the administrative capital, was a small colonial settlement fifteen kilometres (some ten miles) distant. Most of the colony's economic activity was focused in the west, at Takoradi, the only port along the coast with a deep harbour and the departure point for shipments of cocoa, gold, diamonds, manganese, palm oil and rough timber. The Gold Coast was then the most prized of Britain's African colonies and the lofty white walls of no fewer than thirty-one fortresses still tower over the Atlantic Ocean along this stretch of coastline, where the Portuguese landed in 1471.

Three generations of coffin-makers: (top left) Ata Owoo (1904–1976), who founded the business; (top right) a portrait of Kane Kwei (1922–1992) which still hangs in the workshop of his son Sowah (born 1954), seen (bottom right) standing behind a cockerel; (bottom left) Paa Joe (born 1945), Kane Kwei's nephew, posing behind a lion.

The Spirit of the Coast

The arrival of the Portuguese in 1471 coincided with the last of Africa's great tribal migrations and the birth of the coastal and interior states. From the west came a group of tribes called the Akan. The first of these, the Guan, followed the course of the Volta and settled in the hills around Akwapim, north-east of Accra, in about 1300. Then came the Fante, who travelled down the Tano valley, reaching the coast in the region of Cape Coast. The Ashanti (to whom we owe the first villages built of banco, a type of adobe) settled in the wooded hills of the Obuasi region in around 1550. The Ga, originally from Benin and Yorubaland, came along the coast from the east, travelling either on foot or in pirogues, and occupied the plains around Accra in about 1500. They were followed much later, in the 18th century, by the Ewe. Historical documents trace the origins of the Akan back to the ancient empire of Ghana, neighbouring the Malinke empire (Mali), which controlled almost the whole of western Africa from the 13th to the 16th centuries.

Soon after the Portuguese arrived in the 15th century, Holland, England, Sweden, Denmark and even Brandenburg followed suit, bringing major disruption to the economic and social fabric of the region. The country turned now towards the sea, receiving European merchandise and beliefs in exchange for gold and slaves. As Jean Rouch writes in *Migrations au Ghana (Gold Coast),*[5] 'And so the end of the 15th century witnessed a new phenomenon: "the spirit of the Coast", whereby a whole section of Africa turned its back on Africa.'

The story was the same along the whole of West Africa's southern coast, but thanks to the gold that gave this stretch of the coastline its name, European forts sprang up here in far greater numbers than elsewhere. From the end of the 19th century the English established themselves as the dominant power in the region, ousting the other European nations one by one, either buying them out or taking their trading posts by force.

James Moxon, Pram-Pram district commissioner. In 1943 he was responsible for bringing the first radio to this Ga village, which lies to the east of Teshi.

After Pearl Harbour

When Kane Kwei left Teshi in 1937, he was not to return for another ten years. He spent those ten years cutting wood in the Ashanti forests in the heart of the country, learning to distinguish the white woods such as wawa, niangon and okoume, used in standard carpentry jobs, from iroko or bilinga, which were more suitable for any kind of building exposed to damp. Azole was a particularly resilient wood which did not split easily and was resistant to vibration and shock, qualities that made it ideal for aircraft construction. With the onset of the Second World War, demand for this type of wood increased enormously.

The Americans left their mark on Teshi and, on his return in 1947, Kane Kwei barely recognized his native place. It was surrounded by vast military camps, which stretched all the way to the capital. On the hill overlooking the township planes took off and landed daily. There were other differences too: the British no longer wore their colonial-style topees, and wherever he went, Kane heard jazz playing. With the construction of the camps, carpentry workshops had sprung up everywhere, and some of these were now equipped with a mechanical lathe, including his brother Adjetei's, which had changed its name to the DDA Furniture Workshop.

James Moxon, the new British colonial administrator, gave further evidence of the changes brought about by the war. 'After Pearl Harbour,' he commented, 'American planes arrived on the Gold Coast like flights of migrating birds. Accra became a stopover for the Allied supply lines destined for North Africa. The planes flew from the US to Pernambuco in Brazil, then crossed the Atlantic, touching down at Ascension, then Accra, Maiduguri, El Fashir in the Sudan and finally Cairo. At Accra the Americans built a luxurious "township" with hot and cold water and a drainage system leading to the sea. Their presence thoroughly changed life in the town. The British used to pretend that the African quarter, or "downtown" as it was known, simply did not exist, and the only Englishmen the Ghanaians ever saw were the soldiers in their topees pulled down over their eyes. For the thousand American servicemen stationed here, on the other hand, "downtown" was Real Life, and these lads used to wander about at all hours of the day wearing little more than a pair of shorts and a T-shirt and nothing at all on their heads. The myth of the white man was dead!'

Kane Kwei's brother, Kane Adjetei, helped to build the American camps. He told me that it was the first time he ever saw white men working with their hands.

Grandmother's Aeroplane

Kane Kwei and Adjetei's grandmother died in 1951 at the age of ninety-one, and the two brothers made her coffin, designing it in the shape of an aeroplane. She had never travelled by plane, of course, but after the airport was built she used to say that she often daydreamed about flying.

Since the end of the war, on important public occasions Teshi's traditional chief, or *mantse*, had ridden in a palanquin[6] shaped like an eagle. Ata Owoo's workshop, the largest in Teshi (employing forty or more apprentices), had designed and built the palanquin, which so impressed the headman of a neighbouring village that he ordered one for himself in the shape of a cocoa pod. (Ghana was the world's biggest exporter of cocoa beans at this time.) The chief never got to ride in his palanquin, dying before it was completed, and the cocoa pod served him as a coffin instead.

Ata Owoo's cocoa pod gave the Kane brothers the idea of building their grandmother's coffin in the shape of an aeroplane. The other members of their clan were so taken with the aeroplane when it was finished that Kane Kwei, encouraged by Ata Owoo, decided to devote himself exclusively to this type of work.

Ata Owoo was born in 1904 and had trained virtually all the other carpenters in the region. According to his children and his contemporaries, he brought real artistic talent to his job, devoting his spare time to making ornamental wooden sculptures for interiors, church furnishings and coffins. In the 1930s he had sculpted a locomotive engine and a series of carriages which were used as props by a travelling theatre. On his death in 1976 he gave the magnificent two-storeyed house he had built (the Ga's supreme symbol of success)[7] to the Jehovah's Witnesses.

Ata Owoo's workshop had occasionally produced palanquins and coffins in the shape of eagles or cocoa pods, but it was through Kane Kwei's efforts that the idea evolved into a new art form. In 1951 he opened a workshop behind his wife's house in the heart of old Teshi. Employing only one apprentice, a giant of a man called Denfu, he worked in relative privacy and almost exclusively for the elders of his clan. The second coffin he made, a pirogue designed for launching at high tide, was for one of his uncles who owned a whole fleet of such boats. The pirogue was representative of Kane's whole approach, and in response to the Ga's varying requirements, he began reproducing objects that were symbolic of worldly success and elevated social status – pirogues and fish, cows, corn cobs, onions, peppers or houses, depending on whether the coffin was for the family of a wealthy fisherman or a cattle breeder or a crop farmer. Kane Kwei never made preliminary sketches for his coffins, simply drawing the three-hundred-odd elements of the design straight on to the wood. He would throw away sections with which he was dissatisfied, in a constant endeavour to make the shapes more lifelike.

In 1960 Kane Kwei took on one of his nephews, Paa Joe, as an apprentice. Today Paa Joe is his most distinguished successor.

Paa Joe

Paa Joe had been living with his father in a Ga farming colony up in the Akwapim hills, north-east of Accra, but had found the harshness of the life intolerable and, in 1960, at the age of fifteen, he had run away to rejoin his mother in Teshi. Like all Ga, he regarded his mother's concession as his real home.

Paa Joe's mother placed him as an apprentice with his carpenter cousin Kane Kwei. As a member of Teshi's wealthiest clan, the Agbawe, Kane was in a position to live from his art and he was already working exclusively on figurative coffins at this time. While he was learning his craft Paa Joe received his board, but no wage. He himself refers to this period as 'after the departure of the Whites and prior to the construction of the Akosombo dam', in other words, between 1957 and 1963, the year that a dam was constructed on the River Volta – an event whose repercussions appear to have affected the Ga even more profoundly than independence itself. The construction of the Akosombo dam turned Ghana into an industrialized nation, marking the high point in the career of Dr Kwame Nkrumah, founding father of the new republic and its first president.

Ata Owoo made this eagle palanquin for the Teshi chief Nii Ashitey Akomfra III (1902–1977) after the Second World War. The palanquin had both a practical use and the added advantage of glorifying its owner while he was still alive; not surprisingly, it started quite a craze. This photograph was taken in Teshi in 1957 at the time of independence.

Apprentices posing in front of their masterpieces. Their eagerness to be photographed is understandable, given how short-lived these works of art are.

Of the above six coffins, only one was never intended for actual burial: the Mercedes bearing the registration 'Paa Joe' (top left), made for the Centre Georges Pompidou, Paris, in 1989. Today it belongs to an art gallery in Zurich.

The Road to Teshi

A few years earlier, in 1957, the Gold Coast had become the first colony of Black Africa to achieve independence. Its national reserves totalled £60,000,000 sterling, but the country had no university and only two hospitals. President Nkrumah was responsible for changing its name to Ghana and for building new hospitals and schools (whose number he increased tenfold) and the first universities. The dam on the River Volta, which flows through the Akosombo gorges, was to be the industrial heart of the country. The British in their time had calculated that the river's current could be harnessed to provide electricity for the whole of West Africa, but they were deterred by the cost of the project. When Ghana became independent, Nkrumah succeeded in obtaining financial backing for the new dam from both the United States and the country's former British masters. The Americans were taking a keen interest in Ghana, the first Black African republic, which had a seat in the UN at a time when racial segregation was still a matter of course back home. The construction of the dam, begun in 1961, gave work to tens of thousands of Ghanaians, and hundreds of villages that were going to be submerged had to be rebuilt elsewhere.

Tema, a fishing village near Teshi, midway between Akosombo and the capital, was the site selected for the new port, and with its creation a whole host of small Ghanaian businesses grew up. Inevitably, there was a considerable increase in traffic passing through Teshi on its way to Tema or Akosombo, and Kane Kwei took advantage of this situation by building a house and workshop on the main road, next to the new service station. Paa Joe still whistles with admiration when he describes the consequences of this move: 'We worked night and day! We made Chevrolets, cocoa pods, whales, canoes …'. It was 1962. Lavish burial ceremonies were once the prerogative of tribal chiefs; now any member of a tribe could have one, if his family and friends could afford to pay for it – and what better way of honouring and thanking their fathers for their new-found prosperity?

1962-1972:
Ten Glorious Years. Paa Joe's Story

In describing his cousin as he was then, Paa Joe paints a picture of an expansive, generous man. The workshop apparently received so many commissions that they could scarcely cope with the demand. Kane Kwei had taken on several new apprentices, whom he fed enormous quantities of food and showered with gifts of one sort or another, including clothes. It seems that he was a brilliant conversationalist and often had friends round to drink with him and listen to traditional music. In time his third son, Sowah (born in 1956) and later Annang (born in 1965) trained in the family business. Paa Joe and three of Kane's other apprentices, Laï, Té and Paa Willy, were eventually to start up their own businesses at different locations along the coast. In 1972 Paa Joe gave back to Kane 1 bottle of gin, 1 bottle of whisky, 12 yards of Adinkra cloth, 24 bottles of beer, 1 pair of sandals, 1 goat and 50 cedis (a considerable amount of money then), so returning, like for like, all the presents he had received from Kane during his twelve-year apprenticeship. He also agreed to carry on working for another two years without pay, during which time Kane continued to make new models, including his first, highly successful, crayfish.

In 1973 the workshop received a visit from an American lady[8] who owned a gallery in Los Angeles. The woman was so taken by Kane's creations that she put in an order for seven coffins for display in her gallery. Paa Joe and the apprentices made the seven coffins in record time. In order to speed things up, Kane sent the American lady an eagle that had already been made for a local funeral, and Paa Joe had to spend the next two days and an entire night making another eagle for the impatient relatives. Kane took his whole team to the local hotel to celebrate the American sale, but gave Paa Joe nothing for his efforts. It was this incident which persuaded Paa Joe to leave his master and get a job at the Yao Yartel shipyard, which was said to make the best trawlers along the coast. Paa Joe worked there for four years and then returned to Teshi to start up his own coffin-making business. His first commission was a coffin in the shape of a house.

Teshi, 1992

Ghana, like the rest of Africa, experienced rapid economic decline after 1975, but the economic climate had little impact on Kane's business, since, as he said himself, 'all a dead person owns is his coffin'.

He had originally made his coffins out of mahogany but had since replaced this with wawa, a much lighter, white wood which had the added advantage of being easier to work. Each coffin requires six to eight planks two and a half metres (about eight feet) in length. When I visited his workshop in 1992, four apprentices aged between twelve and eighteen were working under a corrugated-iron roof behind his shed, sawing, planing and nailing sections of wood in accordance with Kane's instructions. They were making a chicken for a group of children who had lost their mother, a 'particularly worthy woman', as Kane told me, who had set herself up in business in order to pay for her eight children to receive an education. Kane showed me a number of small pieces of wood in the shape of stylized chicks which he was intending to nail around the chicken's feet to represent the children. A ninth, placed 'a little behind the others', was to represent the woman's first-born, which had died.

The apprentices had no plan or sketch to work from; Kane simply drew the most elaborate sections of the design directly on to the wood. Their only implements, apart from a hammer, were a saw, a plane, a chisel, a razorblade and some sandpaper. They assembled the carved sections with the help of nails under Kane's guidance – the usual practice in the workshop. At one end of the chicken's body (which was still only an oblong box at this stage) the young lads attached the bird's neck. On top of this they superimposed five triangular sections, with their points facing forwards, to form a block of wood in which they carved the beak and the head, using first the saw, then the plane. They finished off the rounded areas using a razorblade, then sandpapered the whole creature until any unevenness had been smoothed out to Kane's satisfaction. The chicken was then ready to be painted.

The Last Commission

Kane Kwei pretended not to notice the three men crossing his courtyard with a vague greeting apparently intended for no one in particular. He left it up to his youngest son, Annang, to go over and ask whât they wanted. Annang listened to the youngest of the three men, then, nodding his head, came over to his father. The men wanted 'a bible' for their dead father-in-law, he said. Kane got up and went into the display room, signalling to the others to follow him. Stationing himself between the canoe and the cocoa pod, he mumbled a figure to Annang, who repeated it in a loud voice – 30,000 cedis. The man who appeared to be acting as spokesman for the others thought for a moment, then said: 'Your father knew Seth, the dead man. Can't he give us a better price in memory of him?' Annang was about to repeat what the man had said, but Kane cut him short with an impatient gesture. 'That's what people always say', he declared. 'I'd have to shut up shop if I gave special prices to friends. And what help will I get from them when I'm ruined?' 'Come on, that's not what we meant,' the man replied, 'but we've only got 25,000 cedis on us.' 'That's too bad', said Kane. 'You can take it or leave it. Look at these coffins here: they can spend the whole year in the workshop. It's all the same to me. They don't eat; they don't cost me anything. A price is a price!' The men finally agreed and received an assurance that the bible would be ready in three days.

When they had left, Kane explained that the bible was an easy model to produce and the only one that was acceptable to the Church. 'None of the others are,' he said, 'because they're carried through the streets, and at the burial itself people sometimes perform animist rituals and animal sacrifices, both of which are prohibited by the Church.'

In 1992 Kane's annual turnover was about thirty coffins. 'Some of them are ordered in advance, for people who are still alive', he told me. 'The family decides what shape the coffin should have, though the old folk sometimes make their preferences known before they die. But' – in answer to my query – 'I have never ever known of anyone ordering their own coffin.' Asked what sort of coffin he would like to be buried in himself, Kane laughed and said: 'Once I'm in the other world, it won't be my responsiblity. I'll go in whatever I'm given.'

When he was approaching fifty, Kane became a Methodist under the influence of his second wife. When he died, in July 1992, Paa Joe built him a coffin to which the Teshi Methodists could not possibly object. He gave it a traditional rectangular shape and – his one concession to Kane's former trade – nailed four small wooden objects – a saw, a hammer, a chisel and a set square – at each of the four corners.

Kane's sons had just finished a job for an art gallery in California, and they and their latest emblems – a tiger, a cow, a crab, a lobster, a Mercedes Benz, an outboard motor and a pirogue – escorted their father's coffin from church to cemetery.

Apprentices at work (this page and opposite). This method of sawing (top right) by pushing the saw away from the body dates back to the 19th century, when Swiss and German carpenters, members of the Basel Mission, built the first missions in the country and trained local carpenters in their techniques.

Apprentices receive food but no wages. They are taken on at an early age and the majority try to set up their own simple carpentry business by about the age of sixteen; not all, however, will go on to become master craftsmen.

23

A Death at Botianaw

In 1987, on the third Thursday in July, at sunrise the women of the village of Botianaw were waiting on the beach for the pirogues to return. Efua, a child of twelve, was drawing water from the stream that flows behind the village. When she reached the women's concession she emptied her bowl into two buckets and put the water on the fire to heat. One bucket was for her father, who would soon be back from fishing, and the other she would take to old Tse.

Tse was in charge of the men's concession of the Obaneh clan, which had as many pirogues as all the other clans of the village put together. As the oldest inhabitant of Botianaw, Tse was held in great respect by all the other villagers.

At dawn the men's concession was empty. Fishing nets hung from the courtyard walls waiting to be mended, and the yard itself, with the living quarters leading off it, was spotlessly clean. Efua knew that she would find Tse sitting on his bench smoking in front of the 'founder's' room. This was originally a simple hut, erected a hundred and fifty years earlier by Tse's grandfather, who now lay buried under the floor. Over the years other huts had been built alongside the first, forming the square compound, with its dozen or so rooms, that Efua had always known. The little girl loved the neatness and order of the empty yard. The women's concession, by contrast, was always cluttered with cooking pots and blackened by smoke from the fires on which the fishermen's meals were prepared, since on land the men never prepared their own food.

Tse was not on his bench. Efua knocked at the old man's door, announcing her arrival with the hot water. She knocked and called out again several times, but got no response, so she finally pushed the door open. Tse was stretched out on the bed with his eyes staring and his mouth wide open, and flies were clustering at the corners of his lips. Efua closed the door and hurried back to the women's concession, where her sisters were crushing chillies to put in the *shito*, the morning meal of fermented maize and smoked fish. Without a word, she put down her bucket and ran to the beach to find her mother, to whom she confided the news in a low voice.

Once the fish had been unloaded and the pirogues pulled up on to the beach, Tse Obaneh's children and brothers assembled in the dead man's room. They cut off a lock of his hair and a few nail parings, then wrapped the body in a sheet and loaded it on to the family truck, which was bound for the market in Accra, twelve kilometres (seven and a half miles) away, to deliver the morning catch. They were thus able to avoid making an unnecessary journey, since the morgue was on the outskirts of the capital.

Once the truck had left, a heated debate began regarding the funeral expenses. Tse's funeral service had to be representative of his status as clan elder and of his extraordinary success as both fisherman and farmer. His death, at over eighty, would be celebrated moreover as the victory of a man who had attained the status of an ancestor.[9] Any members of the clan who were away from home would have to be told the news, and the burial delayed until their return. Meanwhile, the body would have to be kept at the morgue, involving further expense. The family agreed that the burial should take place in three weeks' time, on the second Saturday in August (with the wake starting twenty-four hours prior to this). They also agreed that Tse had died 'Nyomon's death', in other words, of natural causes, and that it would not therefore be necessary to interrogate the body regarding possible revenge.

As the eldest of Tse's sons-in-law, Teteh was traditionally responsible for paying for the coffin, and he suggested one in the shape of an onion. Tse's youngest daughter, whose great dream was to live in town, proposed a Mercedes, the old man's favourite car and the most prestigious symbol of his wealth. Sowah, one of Tse's brothers, favoured a tuna, a fish that Tse had excelled at catching in his youth. In the end the family opted for the onion. Thirty years earlier Tse had handed over his fleet of pirogues to one of his younger brothers and had made a fortune growing onions, an essential ingredient of the Ga diet.

Along with the large quantities of beer and spirits that were an indispensable part of any funeral service, the coffin constituted the major expense. Only Manko, the oldest of the men present, raised an objection to the additional expense of a dresser-cum-cosmetic artist to prepare the body on the eve of the burial. Manko reminded the others that in his time the village women used to do this themselves. When it came to sewing up the dead person's lips, however, there were no longer many village women eager to volunteer for the job, and in the end the family decided to employ a professional dresser. The same woman would be responsible for providing the ceremonial bed on which the dead man would lie during the wake.

Each member of the family offered to look out a good photograph of the dead man for the obituary notice, fifty or so copies of which would be stuck up in the neighbourhood of the village; a copy would also appear in the national newspaper. It was the job of Tse's daughters to go to the market in Accra to choose the dead man's funeral clothes (three different sets) and the cloth for the women to wear at the wake and the funeral. They would also use the occasion to hire a sound system for the dancing.

The provisional list of expenses for Tse's funeral ran as follows: embalming 5,000 c; morgue 75,000 c; coffin 80,000 c; drink 80,000 c; cloth 50,000 c; obituary notice 10,000 c; announcement in the press 20,000 c; ceremonial bed 10,000 c; dresser's fee 9,000 c; transport 7,000 c. The total came to 346,000 cedis, a figure equivalent to three or four years' income for a peasant and more than two years' wages for a town-dweller. From Friday to Sunday families and sometimes whole tribes are on the move, travelling to distant funeral locations, where vast sums of money are spent. Life in Ghana is conditioned by this fact. A business can cease to function from Friday morning while employees make their way in convoy to the native village of a dead colleague. Younger people are buried at less expense, but the sums spent on a burial are always greater than those devoted to health. No one wants to miss a funeral and everyone contributes financially in the knowledge that they will receive the same glorious send-off when their turn comes. Ghanaian families contribute to what can only be described as the dead person's tontine,[10] since the funeral service brings in from friends and members of the clan sums equal to, and sometimes in excess of, those they have spent themselves.

Dzee Ya Se! It's Dark. Be Off!

Every Friday morning the roads around Korle Bu, Accra's morgue, are blocked with lines of the local *tro-tro*, painted wooden trucks bearing slogans declaring *The Poor Man Has No Friend*, *In the End the Tomb*, or *Let Them Speak*. Whole families pile out of these gaudy vehicles and assemble in two large covered areas giving on to the central yard. Only the spouses and children actually enter the building to reclaim the body. It is dark inside, and the air is cool and damp, smelling strongly of the women's perfume. Each time a body is wheeled out there is a new outburst of sobbing. The members of the family crowd round the dead person. They lay the body out on a stretcher brought for the purpose and cover it with a piece of multicoloured cloth, leaving the face free. The men, who alone refrain from weeping, sing a few verses of their tribal song in loud voices, and whenever they name the dead person they add the words 'Dzee Ya se! It's dark. Be off!'

It is August 1987. We are at Korle Bu. Tse Obaneh's body has just been lifted into the Botianaw fishermen's *tro-tro* amid much weeping. An argument between the dead man's sons and his brothers as to whether to place his head towards the front of the vehicle (as the sons wished) or towards the rear (his brothers' wish) was resolved in favour of the sons. The twenty or so men crammed in on either side of the stretcher, which was placed on the floor of the vehicle, and as soon as the lorry started to move they began singing their clan's war songs. Tse's two wives fanned his face in silence to chase away the flies. When the *tro-tro* reached Botianaw's central street, the songs boomed out louder than ever and the entire population of the village crowded round the vehicle. Wails mixed with the songs of the Asafo, companies of young warriors with their heads beribboned in red who fired blank shots from their ancestors' rusty old rifles, scattering children, chickens and goats in the process. Weeping women opened up a path through the crowd by beating the ground with lengths of cloth and Tse was carried to his room. On the threshold a sacrificed chicken lay dying while short drum rolls accompanied its death throes.

A degree of calm returned then for a while. Vast awnings had been hung between the joint concessions, and beneath these the women and children set up rows of benches, leaving an open space in front of the dead man's room. Inside Tse lay on his hired double bed with its chromium-plated bedhead and the old village women were helping Mama Kole, the dresser, to sew up the dead man's lips and make up his face. They dressed him in a luxurious embroidered gown, its white silk shining in the neon light from the ceiling, and Mama Kole asked for some old newspapers, sheets of which she crumpled into balls and slid under the silk gown to give it extra volume. She demanded a glass of beer, which she downed in one gulp, and then she put white gloves on Tse's hands and slipped over the top three gold rings which the old man's senior widow had given her. She arranged three long necklaces over his chest, then stepped back to judge the effect. Amid murmurs of approval from the other women, she made a few delicate adjustments to the contours of the gown. Finally she placed at each corner of the bed a small stand with a bunch of plastic flowers on it (these accessories being included in the cost of hiring the bed).

Outside, an argument had broken out between two fishermen, who had already been celebrating Tse's victory with copious quantities of drink. 'Your Christian prayers are a complete waste of time!' yelled one of them, a thin man with unusually broad feet that looked as if they were glued to the ground. 'And I suppose you think that talking to ancestors and fetishes gets you somewhere, do you?' retorted a heavily built man with a moustache. 'Yes! I believe in the fetish, and my tribal markings prove it. The fetish stops the rain and calms the winds! However much they pray, the Whites always have to wear coats because of the cold. Anyway, you talk to spirits too!' 'I certainly don't!' 'You do! You call on the fetish just like everyone else.' 'That's a downright lie. Ask anyone in my crew. They'll tell you: I've only got one God.' 'Then you're a dead man!' 'No, I'm not.' 'Yes, you are. You've had it!' 'Liar, liar!' yelled the Christian, stamping his foot while a crowd of onlookers screamed with laughter. The two men ended up settling their differences and walked off arm in arm.

Messages from Heaven

All afternoon taxis and other cars crammed full of passengers jolted down the track that connects the main road with the village of Botianaw. Relatives and friends were reunited amid much hand-clapping and laughter, but what noise they made was drowned out by the young Asafo as they strode through the village led by a man striking a gong and another blowing a trumpet.

The celebrations in homage of the old man were due to begin that night and as dusk fell the excitement mounted. The village elders sat in front of the death chamber to greet the new arrivals, who then walked over to a table set a little apart from the rest of the proceedings. Here they handed over some silver, while the amount of the gift and the donor's name were carefully noted in the funeral book. Some also gave bank notes, and these were piling up in a basin, which was covered again after each new donation was deposited in it.

A little before midnight the doors and windows of Tse's room were opened, precipitating a mad scramble as the men and women hurriedly formed themselves into a procession. Shouting and crying, they then began to file past the dead man, addressing and berating him. 'You who leave behind your children, don't touch them, don't show yourself to them again, but protect them for ever!' roared one of Tse's brothers. 'Aunt Oku knew about fertility. Ask her to preserve mine!' yelled a young girl. 'You know how to talk to the nets, so fill ours for us!' someone else demanded.

Others thanked the dead man for sums of money borrowed and never paid back or for the food that he had given the more destitute members of the clan. Each reference to his generosity provoked tears from the women and cries of regret, and the old men shouted out his achievements at the top of their voices – how he had built up his fishing fleet and how his subsequent farming successes had benefited the entire village. During the night members of other clans came to pay homage to the dead man, uncorking numerous bottles of spirits and pouring libations before his funeral bed, then striking up war songs. The sound of drums from neighbouring courtyards mixed with the gospel music blaring out from four powerful loudspeakers, while young girls handed round beer and generous portions of rice and fish. An area had been reserved for dancing and all night it was packed; all night children mingled freely with the dancers.

There was a lull between dawn and midday when the celebrants crept off to sleep in the corner of a room or on a bench.

In the Onion

At midday the elders announced that in two hours' time the villagers would have their last glimpse of the dead man before his body was entrusted to the earth. The death chamber became once more the scene of frenetic activity. Over Tse's head an old woman brandished handfuls of banknotes – donations from the guests whose purpose was to pay for the ancestor's passage into the other world. With their drummers in front, the young fishermen marched in procession round the bed and the older men sang the clan song again. Most of the women were sobbing and one of Tse's widows kept addressing the dead man in pathetic tones. The old woman who had been responsible for gathering up the money also appeared to be presiding over the current proceedings. In the midst of all the commotion, she grabbed the other woman by the arm and pointed an accusing finger at the corpse, shouting: 'Tse! She's not your wife any more! Leave her in her world and stay in yours. Don't touch her again and don't show yourself again, even if another man approaches her. Watch over her, instead. It's dark. Be off!' The widow was dragged outside, and through the side door four young men suddenly came in, naked to the waist, bringing with them Paa Joe's work of art, a gigantic green onion. Emotions were reaching fever pitch. The thirty-odd men and women all pressed back against the walls to make room for the coffin. 'Put the onion to the left of the bed!' one person shouted. 'No, to the right!' shouted another. 'Get the women out of here!' demanded one of the fishermen, but was booed into silence. The bizarre construction was finally wedged up against the bed.

'Cover the doors and windows!' someone shouted, and the women immediately held their skirts in front of the openings, where a host of curious faces were bobbing about to get a better view. The lid was removed from the coffin to reveal a lining of white satin. Tse's body was stripped of its jewelry, then placed inside the onion, prompting a frenzy of despair from the family. In an atmosphere of collective hysteria, the onion was then reclosed and nailed down. Four men grasped it by the handles provided on its underside for this purpose and stepped out with it into the courtyard to the accompaniment of cries from the villagers. The bearers pointed the coffin skywards, then lifted it on to their heads.

On its way to the grave, the onion was due to pass through every street in the village, stopping at all the places that had some connection with the dead man's daily life. For a moment it floated above the crowd, describing several circles, unsure which direction to take. Picking up speed, it charged towards a door as if about to break it down, then at the last moment came to a halt, swaying backwards and forwards in front of the owner of the house. The latter addressed the coffin with raised arms and tears pouring down his face. He opened a bottle of gin, sprinkled a few drops on the onion, then poured some into the mouth of each of the bearers in turn. The coffin swung round and charged the crowd, which scattered, shouting, then reassembled at once and followed in hot pursuit as it shot off again through the lanes of the village.

When it was time to change bearers, Tse's grandsons argued over who was to have the honour of carrying the old man. The clan chiefs[11] waited on their doorsteps, waving a bottle of gin or brandy as soon as the coffin came in sight. At repeated intervals the onion would do a half-turn and charge the crowd, then retreat and set off again, encouraged by shouts from the villagers – 'It's dark. Be off!'

When, an hour into this marathon, the onion left the village and struck off into the bushes, only the youngest of the villagers set off in pursuit of it. The adults had already gathered in the open country several hundred metres from the village and were standing round a deep grave dug in the sandy ground. From inside the grave, three men helped to ease down the coffin, whose stem and roots had to be broken off before it would fit into the hole. Despite the women's attempts to stop them, a group of drunken old fishermen were bawling out lewd fishing songs, tacking them on to the end of the clan song. Then the young folk began to cover the coffin, spraying large quantities of sand into the crowd, which dispersed amid shouts of laughter and snatches of drunken singing from the old men. The grave was filled, branches were strewn haphazardly over the top, and suddenly everybody had gone, the place was deserted.

That evening the funeral committee proudly announced that the donations received totalled 422,500 cedis. To thank Tse Obaneh for this last favour, the elders shared a bottle of brandy outside his room, while his eldest son (aged sixty) began moving in his belongings.[12]

For notes to the text, see page 36.

Opposite: Kane Kwei preparing to design a section of a coffin on a plank of wood; three-hundred-odd sections go to make up the finished object. On the wall behind him is his own portrait as a young man.

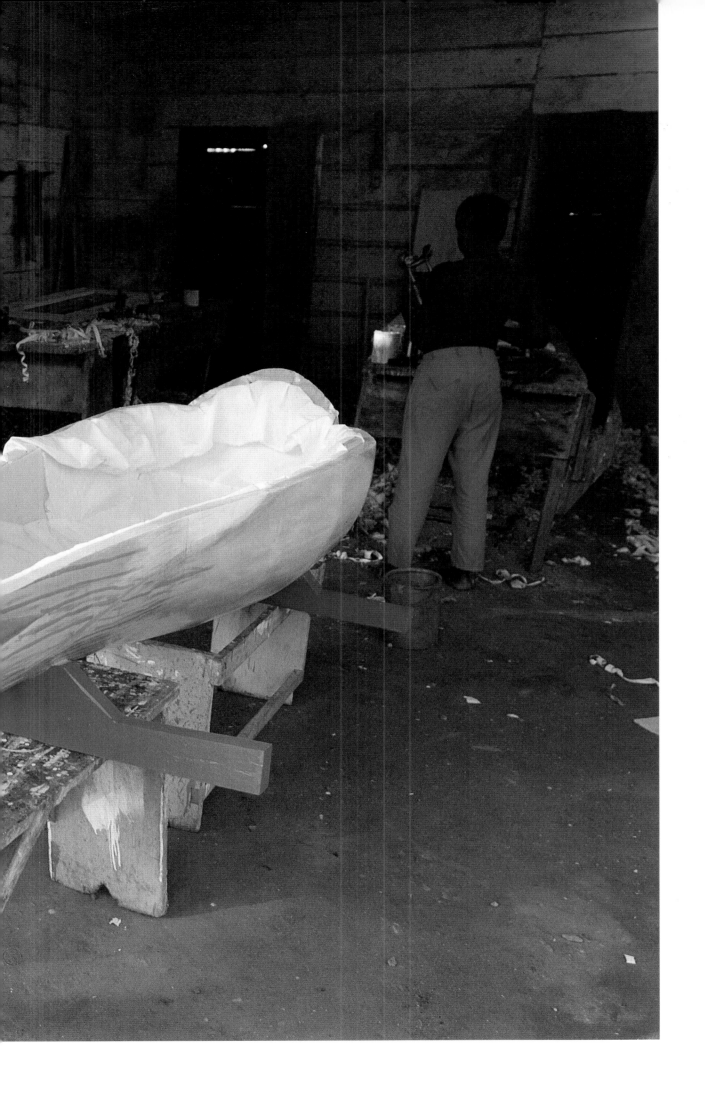

1. When a person dies their soul remains closely linked to their body for three days. The soul then wanders freely for a year until the celebration of the final rite (*faafo*), when it crosses the river into the world of shadows. A person has the same social status in this world as he or she had in life – a chief remains a chief, and a peasant a peasant.

2. In the Ga's ritual songs the supreme god, Sakumo, often assumes the form of an eagle.

3. Ga coffins show similarities with the coffins of the ancient Eleku (in Zaïre), which were shaped like pirogues equipped with bird beaks and decorated with lances, knives, etc. In 1959, however, the ethnologist G. Hulstaert described the Eleku funeral art as an 'art that had long since fallen into disuse' and Kane Kwei could scarcely have drawn his inspiration from it.

4. Even people who spend their entire lives in one of these farming colonies say 'We are from Teshi' or 'We are from Osu.' Once a year they all return to their main township. Accra also has a string of fishing villages attached to it.

5. Jean Rouch, *Migrations au Ghana (Gold Coast)*, CNRS, Paris, 1957.

6. The palanquin was originally a basket in which Akan chiefs (and only they) were transported from place to place. Akan chiefs are known as *nana*, which means both chief and ancestor, since the Akan regard their chiefs as incarnations of their ancestors. When the Ga arrived in the Accra plains in the 16th century, they had a theocratic system of government. They borrowed the concept of secular chiefs, thrones (sacred stools) and palanquins from the Ashanti. In the Ga system, the *mantse* (father of the village) is an assistant priest to whom secular tasks are entrusted in the presence of strangers, and even today the *mantse* takes his orders from the *wulomo* (high priest).

7. A Ga's house is his most valued property, his means of perpetuating his identity, and the Ga believe that a person who builds a house will be remembered longer than any other. His house will bear his name; his children will continue to live in it, and when his descendants die they will lie in the 'founder's' room while others keep watch over their body. It is in this room too that newborn members of the family are baptized.

8. Vivian Burns, *African Arts*, 1974, vol. VII, no. 2, p. 25. Kane Kwei did not mention Ata Owoo to her, although he was still alive at the time. In Burns's short article on Kane Kwei, he says that the first coffin he made was in the shape of a canoe, forgetting to mention the aeroplane which he and Adjetei had made for their grandmother. The precise chronology of these events was established through a series of interviews (recorded between 1987 and 1993) with Kane Kwei himself and with his sons, Kane Adjetei, Paa Joe and former apprentices of Ata Owoo and the latter's children.

9. 'There is an inherent ambivalence in this ancestor worship, since by invoking the protection of a dead person one is also seeking to deflect any angry or vindictive feelings on their part, feelings that are less to be feared from an ordinary person.... The more an individual is in a position to excite envy through his wealth or his power, the more those who survive him will feel the need to appease him and to seek his favour. By envying him, after all, one may be in some degree responsible for his death' (*Rites de la mort*, Musée de l'Homme, Paris, 1981).

10. A system of loans at low rates of interest between the members of a professional body or of a clan. The system, in which the survivors' shares increase as the other subscribers die, is very popular in West Africa.

11. Most of the important members of a Ga township have travelled at some time in their youth and worked in one or other of West Africa's big ports. Some have worked on cargo ships bound for Europe or Asia; others have found employment abroad as farmers or mercenaries. Ex-sailors wear a tattoo on their chest. Rather than being 'detribalized' by these contacts with foreign countries, such travellers tend to show a particular devotion to their township and its traditions and are respected for the experience they have acquired.

12. In the Ga view, genetic inheritance is passed on through the male line. Social status is linked to age, and for both men and women social maturity takes a lifetime to achieve. The first stage is that of physical maturity. When a boy enters this stage, his father gives him a rifle, a symbol linking male status with warrior status. When he marries, a man remains legally a minor until all the preceding generations have died out and the elders of his own generation are also dead. He first assumes authority within his immediate family on the death of his father, and in time this authority extends to the wider family circles.

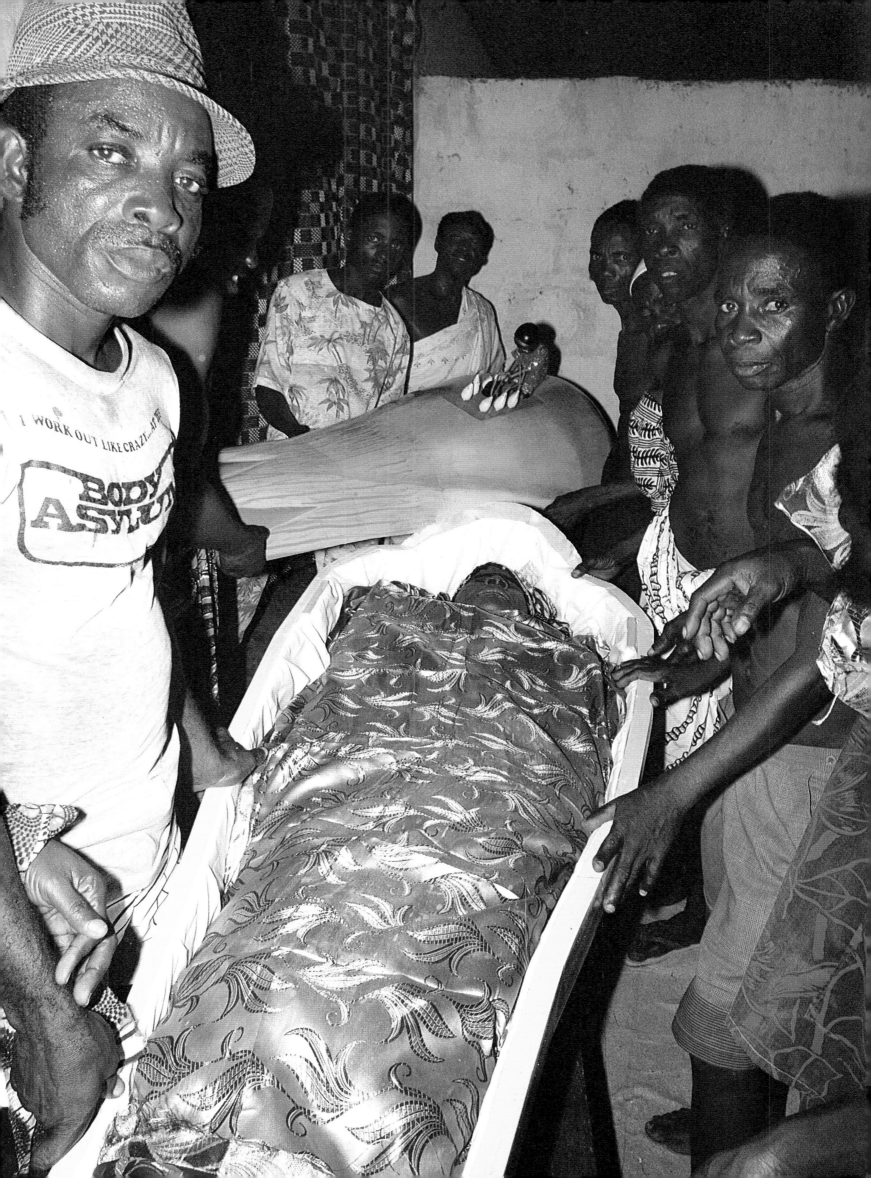

The Cocoa Pod

Nuumo Kwatei Kwaku Nkpa Quartey (1897–1988) was born and buried at Labadi but spent his entire working life at Okorso, Labadi's farming colony on the River Volta, where he grew cocoa.

Cocoa (or cacao), a native of tropical America, was introduced to West Africa in the 19th century. It was first cultivated on the island of Fernando Po (now Bioko) in the Gulf of Guinea and reached the Gold Coast in 1875. Cultivation began in the hills overlooking the Accra plains, and the variety known as 'Accra beans' is still the best today. In 1910 the Gold Coast became the first world producer of cocoa and the colony made a fortune.

The ninety-one-year-old, popularly known as Ataa Aku Nkpa, had lived through a golden age when African planters could be even wealthier than many of their European counterparts, and he had achieved ancestral status in more ways than one – as his burial in the cocoa pod symbolized.

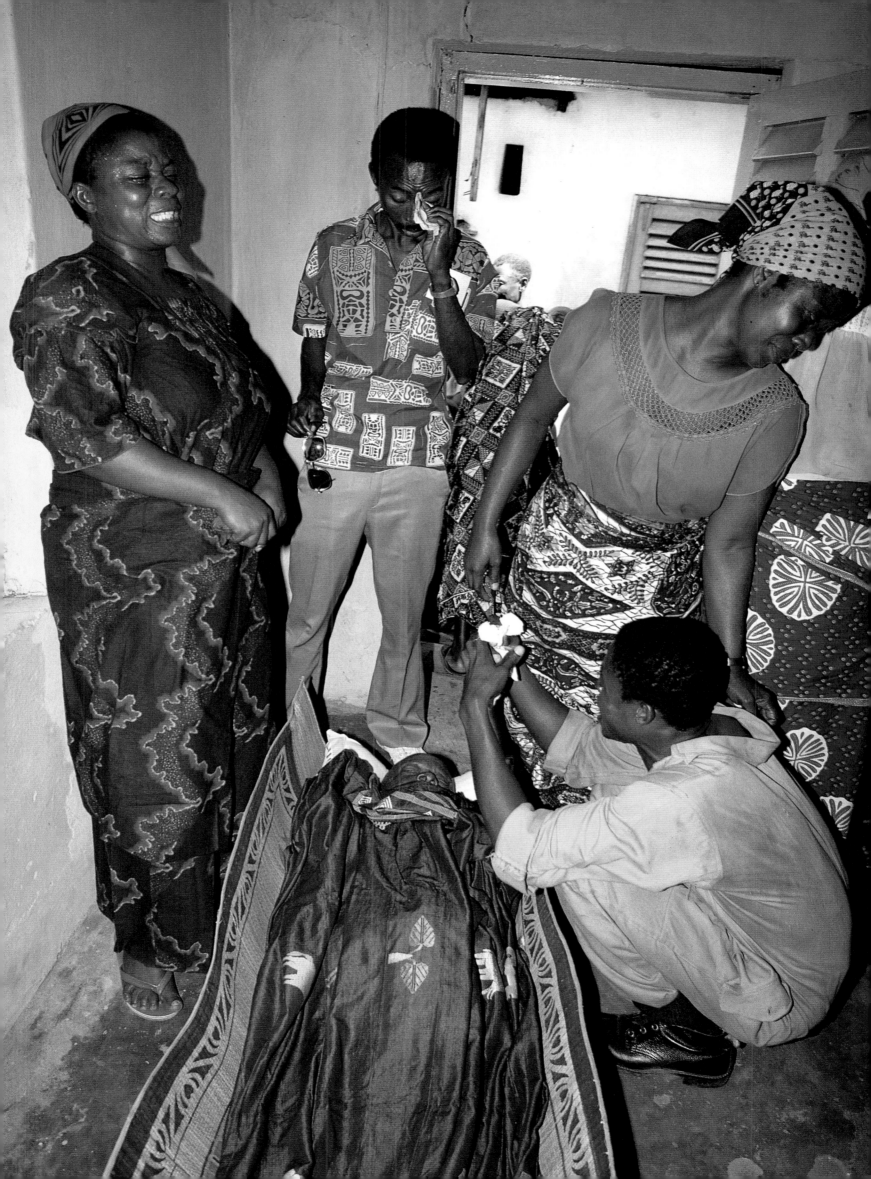

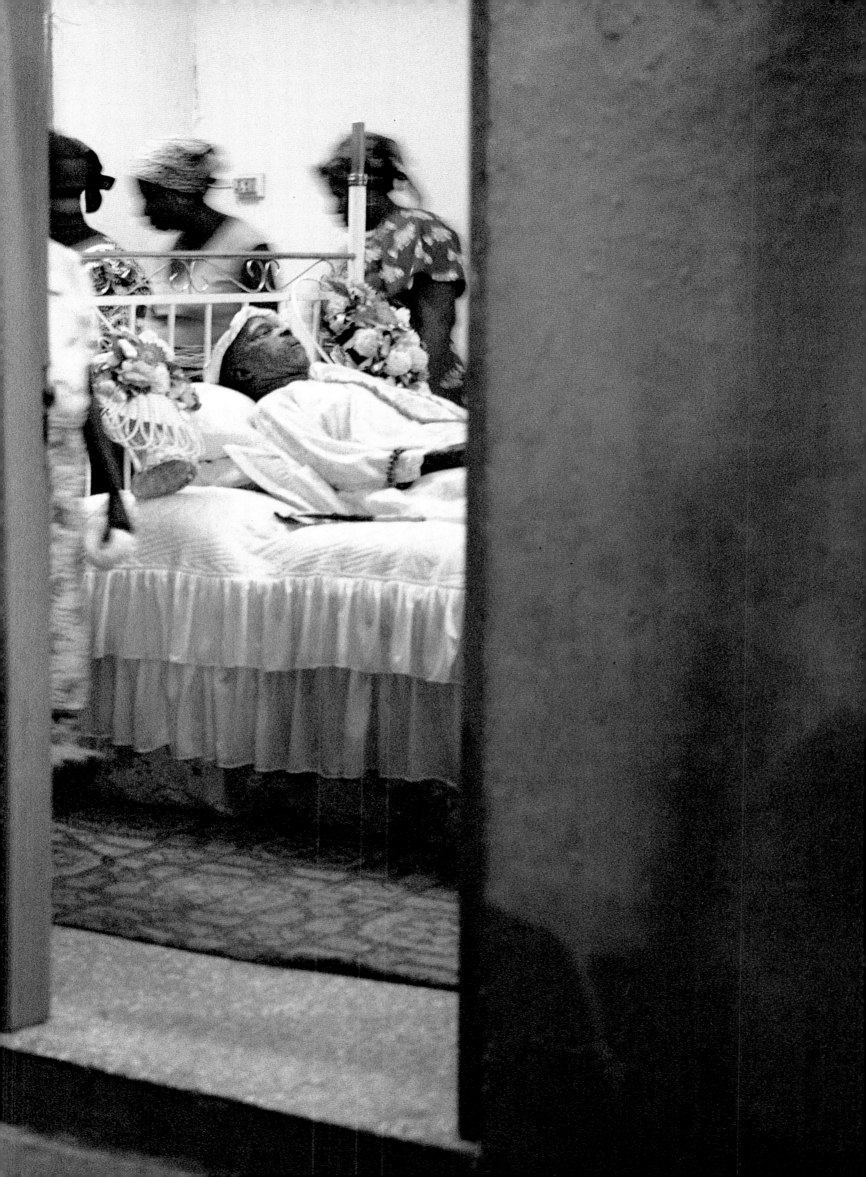

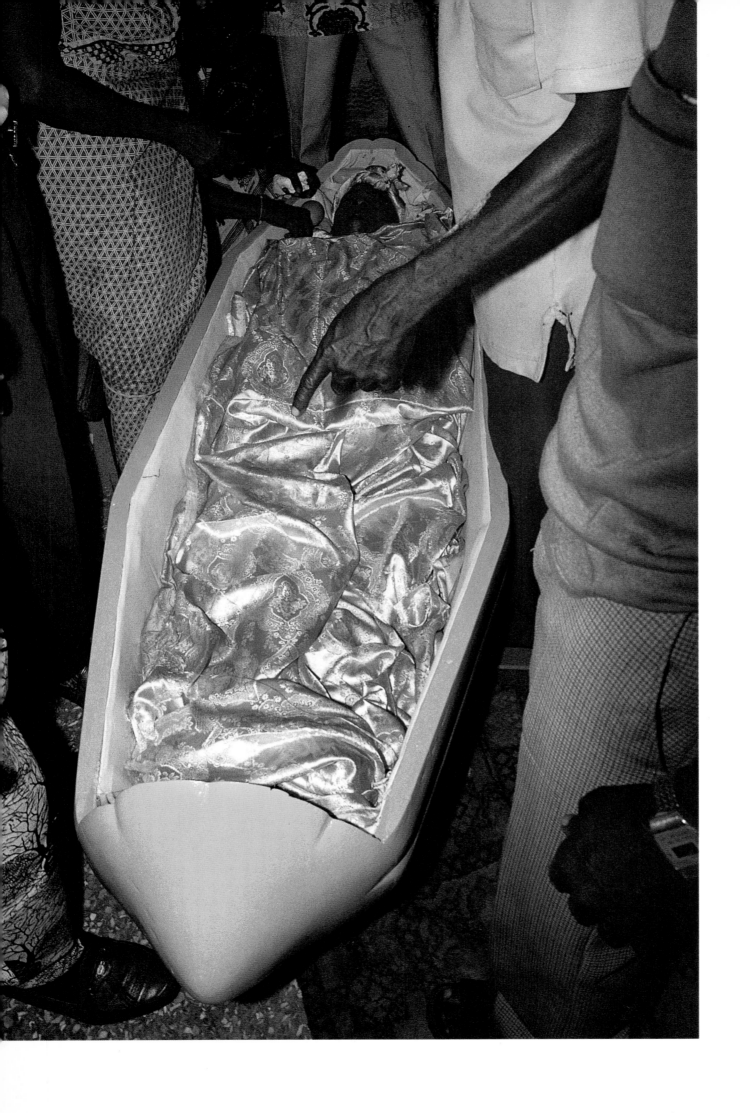

The Sardine

In 1988, a year after Tse Obaneh was buried in an onion at Botianaw, his younger brother was buried in a sardine – the fish he had led expeditions to catch. The prey thus carried off the man.

Tse's brother had been a heavy smoker and the mourners planted a cigarette between his lips for the wake, which took place in the same room – less lavishly decorated on this occasion – in which Tse's body had lain.

The man in charge of fishing at Teshi was also buried in a sardine that year amid particularly noisy and boisterous celebrations. Teshi's fishermen are renowned, in fact, for their vociferous and sometimes brutal enthusiasms. The sardine took two hours to complete its journey under a blistering midday sun, and whenever the route included a section of made-up road the coffin bearers and other barefoot members of the crowd surged forward on the burning tarmac with yells of 'Faster!' Those who were fortunate enough to be wearing shoes just laughed and made snide remarks like 'No need to run. There isn't a fire!' The burial itself, in the dunes behind the beach, provided a perfect opportunity for throwing sand in other people's faces.

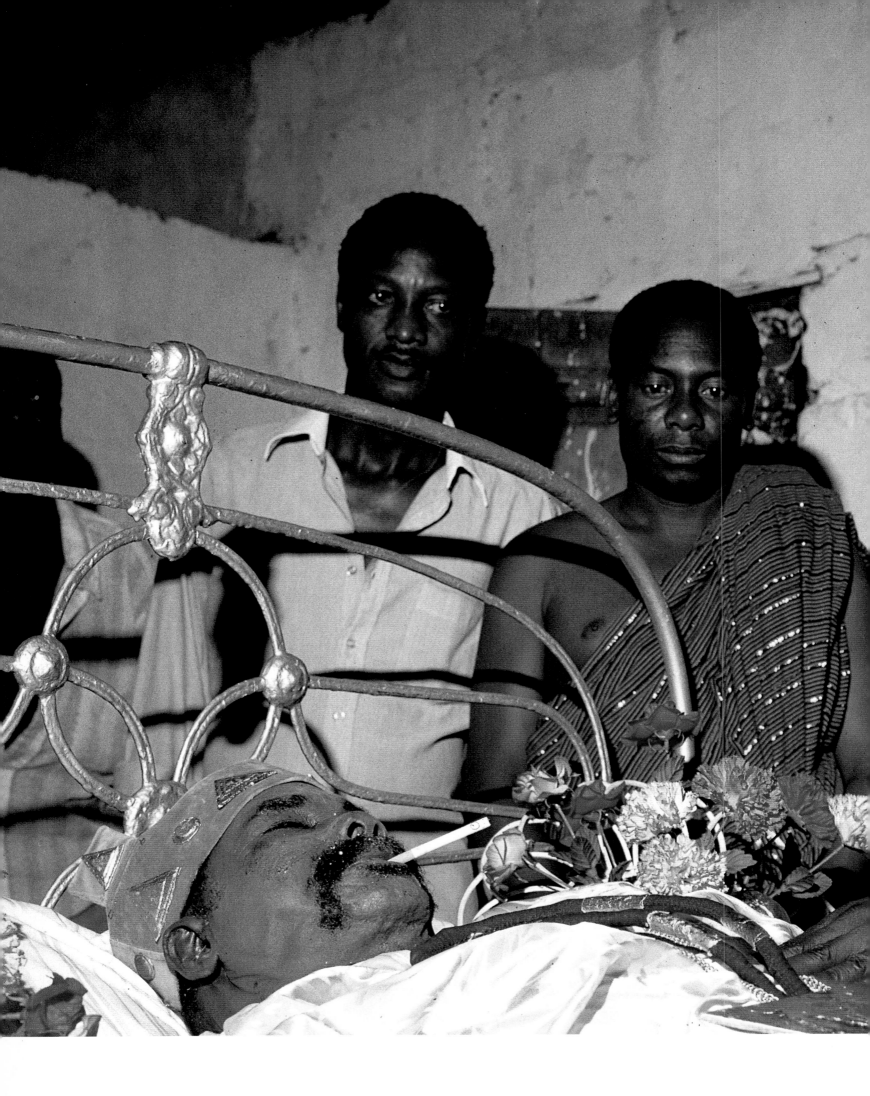

The Pirogue

In 1987 Tsui Tse was buried in a pirogue. He had been the head fisherman at Osu, the oldest of the Ga townships, today a district of Accra. Tsui was born toward the end of the last century, though no one appears to know the precise date: erring on the generous side, his family declared the age of the dead man to be a hundred and one. Tsui had been the guardian of fishing fetishes and all the fetish-women were present at the burial. A young bull was sacrificed for the occasion and the meat was shared out between the members of the family.

A pirogue also served Akoto Apaflo in 1992. The sixty-five-year old was buried at Pute, his native village, near the mouth of the Volta. All of his twenty-two children were present at the funeral, including a number who worked as fishermen in Cameroon (where they owned a fleet of thirty-two pirogues) and who had flown back to Ghana specially.

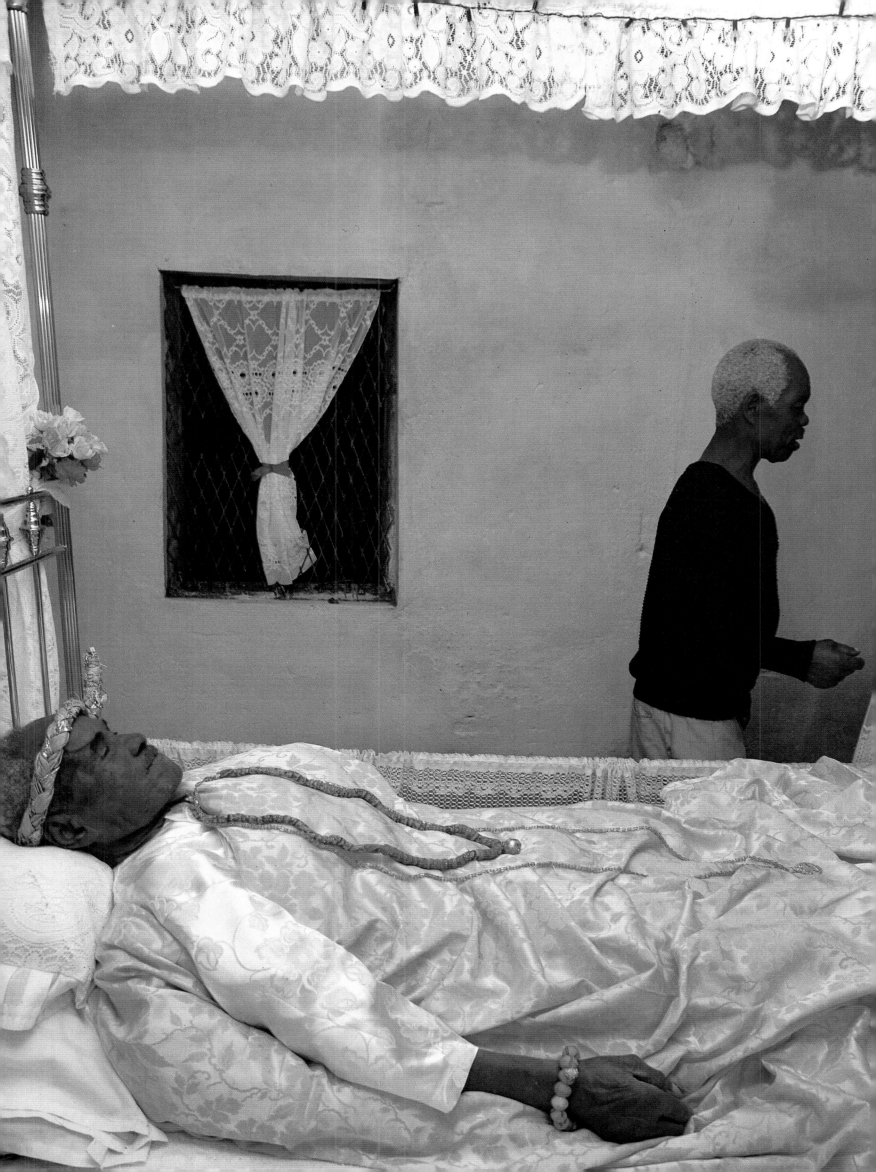

The Eagle

In 1988 Esther Aalakailey Akuetteh, from Labadi, died at the age of ninety and was buried in a golden eagle. She belonged to that fierce class of 'market women' who made their fortune selling on the black market and exchanging contraband goods with Togo and the Ivory Coast. Her other source of income was the Charter Healing Church, which she founded in Labadi with the Reverend Afutu in 1969 with the aim of healing sickness and disability through gospel music and prayer.

Throughout the night before her funeral, the three hundred female members of the congregation (most of them market women like herself) sang gospel songs, and on the morning of the funeral the Reverend Afutu arrived in a Cadillac to conduct the service. At the end of his hour-long sermon he made an appeal for donations and, as the women pressed forward towards the rostrum to hand over their money, he bellowed encouragement into his microphone: 'Sow your money in the kingdom of the Lord and it will multiply! Alleluia!'

The Mercedes Benz

The Mercedes Benz is the ultimate symbol of prestige and wealth in Ghana. Very few people are entitled to be buried in a Mercedes, and because of the great respect their position confers such funerals are always sober affairs with strong Christian overtones.

Since this type of coffin is not allowed inside a church, the religious service is conducted in front of the dead person's house. The coffin is usually given the same registration number as the person's own car, which is sometimes put on display during the wake.

The Chicken

Mary Deddeh Attoh was the oldest woman living in Dansoman, a suburb of Accra. At eighty-five she was still conducting her own business and taking an active part in the affairs of the district.

On her death, in 1987, she left behind eleven children, eighty-two grandchildren and sixty great-grandchildren. Her coffin, made in the shape of a chicken, accordingly had eleven chicks nestling beneath its wings. Mary was a Methodist and her burial service was conducted in a calm, dignified manner after the minister of Dansoman had delivered a funeral oration in the courtyard of the family concession. Kane Kwei's coffins were barred from the church in Dansoman, where the service would otherwise have taken place: for both Protestants and Catholics the use of these coffins smacks of fetishism, which they condemn.

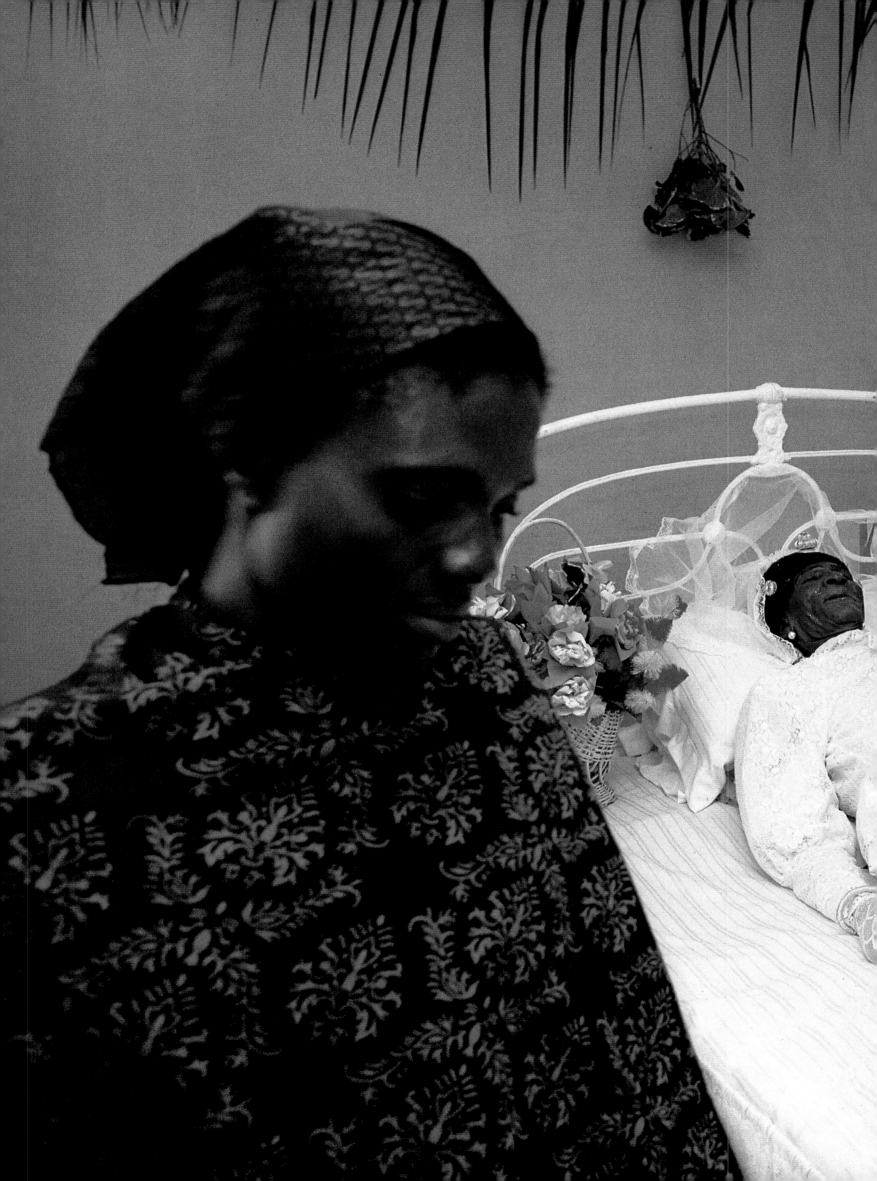

The Lion

The village of Oyarifa lies in the Accra plains, twenty kilometres (about twelve miles) from the coast. It is a typical Ga farming colony, a satellite of Labadi, itself a district of the capital.

Aflache Ayoko (1910–1991) was born and died at Oyarifa, spending his entire life there, hunting in the plains and in the nearby Akwapim hills. In his youth he killed two panthers. In 1983 the region was devastated by huge bush fires and the game was almost completely wiped out.

Aflache's lion-coffin was buried in open country a few kilometres from the village in a pre-prepared grave. On their way to the grave the village elders sang the war song of the Oyarifa hunters, which runs: 'Who wants to fight a lion without good reason? / An animal wanted to fight a lion / We went on. Always the same situation / An uncontrolled fight / Excessive destruction / Who wants to fight a lion without good reason?'

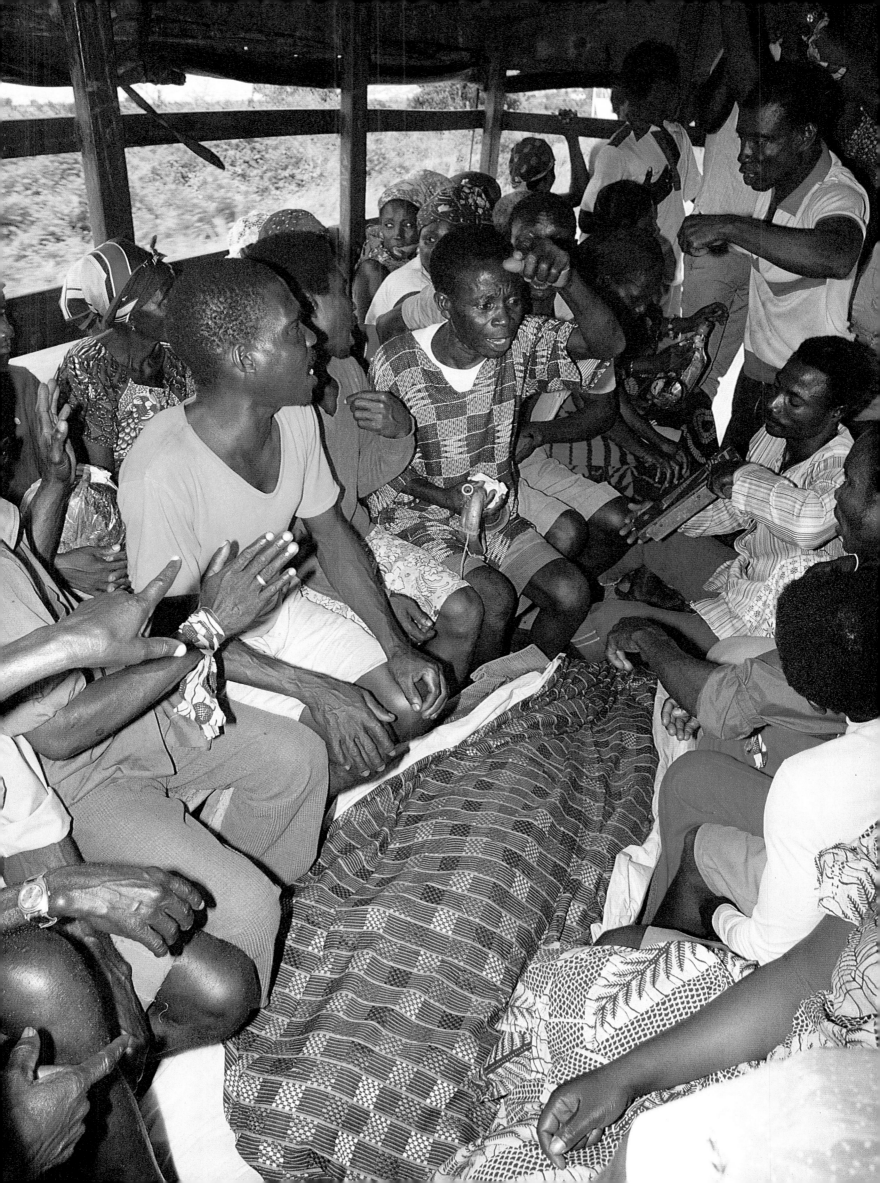

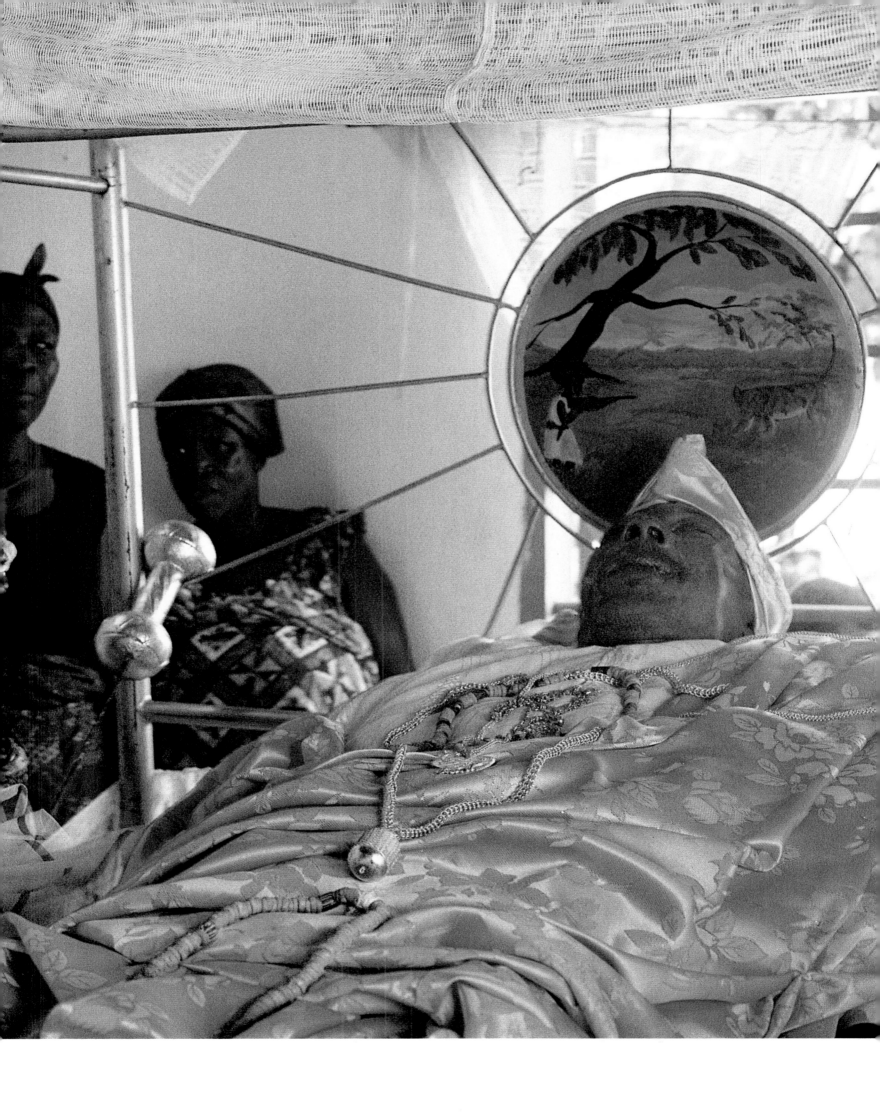

Catalogue of Works

EAGLE
Kane Kwei's workshop.
The 'classic' eagle model, the most popular for clan chiefs. 1992.

EAGLE
Kane Kwei's workshop.
Made by Sowah Kwei. Inspired by the Federal Express symbol. Commissioned by an American gallery. 1992.

ANTELOPE
Palanquin. Paa Joe's workshop.
Made for a chief. 1987.

BUS
Paa Joe's workshop.
Replica of a road haulage contractor's vehicle. 1991.

AEROPLANE
Kane Kwei's workshop.
Made for an international businessman. 1992.

SPORTS BOOT
Sowah Kwei's workshop.
Made for a boxer. 1980.

BIBLE
Paa Joe's workshop.
Made for a minister. 1985.

OIL DRUM
Sowah Kwei's workshop.
Made for a garage owner. 1981.

COCOA POD
Laï's workshop.
Made for a cocoa planter. 1988.

CRAB
Kane Kwei's workshop.
Commissioned by an American gallery. 1992.

DOVE
Kane Kwei's workshop.
Made for a minister. 1992.

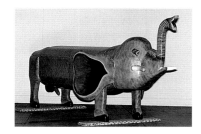

ELEPHANT
Paa Joe's workshop.
Commissioned by the Centre Georges
Pompidou, Paris. 1988.

LION
Paa Joe's workshop.
Made for a hunter. 1991.

PEPPER
Paa Joe's workshop.
Made for a woman who sold
peppers. 1992.

FISHING NET
Paa Joe's workshop.
Exhibition model. 1993.

HOUSE
Kane Kwei's workshop.
Made for a centenarian. 1992.

PIROGUE
Kane Kwei's workshop.
The most popular model with
fishermen. 1992.

CRAYFISH
Kane Kwei's workshop.
Commissioned by an American
gallery. 1992.

MERCEDES BENZ
Paa Joe's workshop.
Exhibition model. 1993.

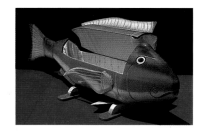

RED FISH
Kane Kwei's workshop.
Made for a fisherman. 1992.

BUTTERFLY
Paa Joe's workshop.
Made for a butterfly collector. 1989.

ONION
Paa Joe's workshop.
Made for an onion grower. 1987.

STRIPED FISH
Kane Kwei's workshop.
Made for a fisherman. 1992.

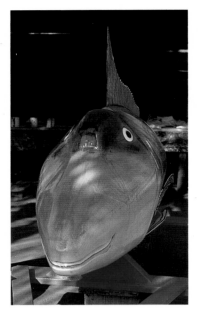

MAUVE FISH
Kane Kwei's workshop.
Made for a fisherman. 1993.

CHICKEN
Kane Kwei's workshop.
One of the most popular models for
women with children. 1988.

PLANE
Paa Joe's workshop.
Made for a carpenter. 1988.

SARDINE
Paa Joe's workshop.
Made for a head fisherman. 1988.

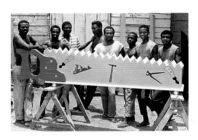

SAW
Kane Kwei's workshop.
Made for a carpenter. 1990.

LEOPARD
Kane Kwei's workshop.
Gbubla, the leopard-god, is sacred
to the Ga.
Commissioned by an American
gallery. 1992.

TROWEL
Paa Joe's workshop.
Made for a builder. 1993.

COW
Kane Kwei's workshop.
Made for a woman who distributed
meat wholesale. 1992.

Acknowledgments

My thanks first of all to Jean-Jacques Mandel, without whom this book would never have come into being, and, of course, to Kane Kwei, his sons and his nephew Paa Joe. I am also grateful to all those Ghanaian families who allowed me to be present and to ask questions during the wake-keeping and the burial of their loved ones, and who tolerated the intrusion of my cameras. I often wonder what sort of welcome a Ghanaian journalist would receive in France if he ambushed mourners at a funeral parlour and asked if he could trot along behind them to their loved one's grave. My thanks also go to those apprentices, village elders, musicians, friends and employees of the Ministry of Information and everyone else who helped to further my research in Ghana: Ben Abdallah, Kwesi Opoku Acheampong, Kane Adjetei, Amah, Tawiah Amah, James Ampadu, Eric Annan, Josuah Armatey, Elvis Aryeh, Haruna Atta, Benham Attar, Azé, Eko Baidoo, Vincent Barker, Dr Barko, Xavier Barral, Batista, Albert Bediako-Boateng, Bill Bell, Jean-François Bizot, Patrick Blossier, Bruno Bodemer, Anne de Boismilon, Patrick Boucher, Annie Boulat, Dominique Boussagol, John Broni, Walter Broni, Jacqueline Brossard, Joyce and Juan Casals, Françoise Chipeaux, Jean Clavet, Eileen Coffee, Dovi and John Collins, Nathan Danquah, Diana, Marie-Sophie Dubus, Marie Dumas, Mathias Fankhauser, Jean-Jacques Flori, Michel Folco, Gabriel and Happy, Gilbert Goldstein, Mary and Louis Graëssli, Eric Guichard, Blaine Harden, Éric Hazan, Bill Hussey, Subi Kalmoni, Ohene Kwame, Annang Kwei, Christina D. T. Kwei, Sowah Kwei, Oheneba Kwame Kyeretwie, Laï, Marianne and Catherine Lamour, Madeleine Le Grèves, Jean-Pierre Ledos, Jean-Luc Léon, Annie and Jean-François Lionnet, Annette Lucas, Marie-Jo, Theodora and Régis Marodon, Béatrice and Jonathan Marshall, Claudine Maugendre, Martin Meissonnier, Jean-Christophe Mitterrand, Etienne Montés, Paul Morris, James Moxon, Bob Nater, P. V. Obeng, Nana Kofi Obonya, Robert Ocran, M. Hodari Okae, Oseï, D. K. Oseï, Teddy Oseï, Edward Prempeh, Prosper, Enianom, Edgar and Winfried Peters, Evelyn Quarshie, Charles Quaye, Nana Konadu Agyemang Rawlings and Jerry John Rawlings, Sheila Reindorf, Denise Rey, Marc Riboud, Jean Rouch, Valerie Sackey, Rita Sackeyfio, Marc Sauvageot, Sylvie and Raymond Secretan, Orlando and Christine Steiger, Tessa Strover, M. Tchokpa, Té, Mac Tontoh, Geneviève Tsegah, Kojo Tsikata, Albert Van Dantzig, Michèle Viard, Otumfo Nana Opoku Ware II, Zacharia, Ian Zebrowski.

Bibliography

Accam, T . N . N .
Dangme and Klama Proverbs
University of Legon, Ghana, 1972

Burns, Vivian
African Arts, Vol. VII, No. 2
Los Angeles, 1974

Dupuis, Annie
Rites de la mort, Catalogue
Musée de l'Homme, Paris, 1981

Field, M . J .
Religion and Medicine of the Ga People
Oxford University Press, 1961

Field, M . J .
Social Organisation of the Ga People
The Crown Agents for the
Colony, London, 1940

Kilson, Marion
African Urban Kinsmen
Hurst and Co., London, 1974

Kilson, Marion
Ga Religious Songs and Symbols
Harvard University Press,
Cambridge, Mass., 1971

Moxon, James
Man's Greatest Lake
André Deutsch, London, 1969

Quarcoo, A. K.
The Lakpa
University of Legon, Ghana, 1963

Rouch, Jean
Migrations au Ghana (Gold Coast)
CNRS, Paris, 1957

Vogel, Susan
Africa Explores
CAA-Prestel, New York
and Munich, 1991